SCHOLASTIC

W9-ANY-645

Success With
Sight Words

New York • Toronto • London • Auckland • Sydney
Mexico City • New Delhi • Hong Kong • Buenos Aires

Teaching *Resources*

State Standards Correlations

To find out how this book helps you meet your state's standards, log on to **www.scholastic.com/ssw**

Cover design by Ka-Yeon Kim-Li
Interior design by Brian LaRossa

ISBN 978-0-545-20112-4

About the Book

A relatively small number of words make up the great majority of text students will come across in the early elementary school years. If students can recognize these high-frequency words at a glance, they will have greater access to all the knowledge that awaits them. The best way to teach sight words is through practice and repetition. This book will help increase familiarity through games and activities designed to boost students' recognition of the top 100 sight words.

Table of Contents

What's Missing?

 Fill in the boxes below to make the list words.

1. t ☐

2. ☐ f

3. a ☐ d

4. ☐

5. ☐ h e

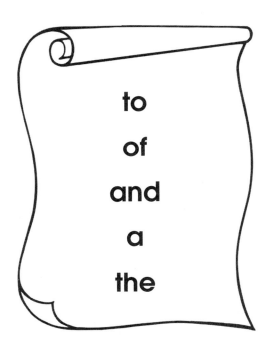

to

of

and

a

the

 Challenge

Fill in the sentences below with list words.

1. We ran out _____ milk.

2. My dog is _____ beagle.

3. My friend _____ I like the same books.

4. I watered _____ plants today.

Hidden Picture

 Color all the shapes that have list words. What picture do you see?

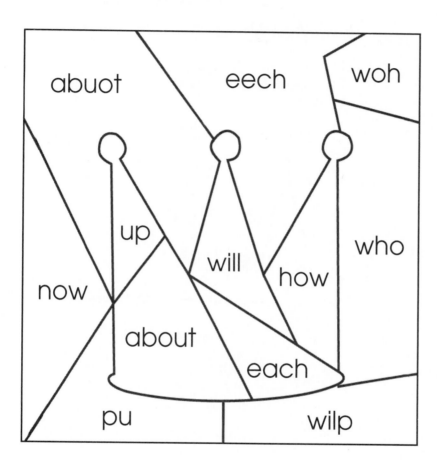

abuot   eech   woh

up

now   will   how   who

about

each

pu   wilp

will

each

about

how

up

Write each word once.

will _____

about _____

up _____

each _____

how _____

Scrambled Words

 Unscramble the letters below to make the list words.

1. uyo __ __ __

2. si __ __

3. ttah __ __ __ __

4. ti __ __

5. ni __ __

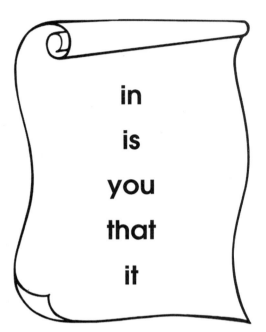

in

is

you

that

it

 Challenge

Use the list words to complete this card.

Thank _____ for the hat. _____

_____ just what I wanted! I hope _____

I will see you _____ the summer.

Name _____

Copy & Circle

 Read each word below. Copy it. Then circle the word in the sentence.

| in |
| is |
| you |
| that |
| it |

Read. Copy. Circle.

1. in   **1.** _____   **1.** My bag was in the car.

2. is   **2.** _____   **2.** His coat is blue.

3. you   **3.** _____   **3.** You can come to my house.

4. that   **4.** _____   **4.** Take that book to school.

5. it   **5.** _____   **5.** I will eat it later.

 Challenge

Circle each of the list words in the story below.

Old Turtles

Did you know that some turtles can live a very long time? One turtle in South America is over 240 years old. It is a very old turtle!

What's Missing?

 Fill in the boxes below to make the list words.

1. w a ☐

2. f ☐ r

3. ☐ r e

4. h ☐

5. ☐ n

he

for

was

on

are

 Challenge

Fill in the sentences below with list words.

1. Yesterday _____ my birthday.

2. You _____ my best friend.

3. I picked some flowers _____ my mom.

4. Tom put _____ his boots.

5. My dad said _____ would help me.

Code Words

 Use this code to write the list words on the lines below.

a ✖   f ★   n ▲   r ●   w ◆

e ♥   h ➤   o ✔   s ■

1. ★ ✔ ●

    ___ ___ ___

2. ✔ ▲

    ___ ___

3. ◆ ✖ ■

    ___ ___ ___

4. ➤ ♥

    ___ ___

5. ✖ ● ♥

    ___ ___ ___

he
for
was
on
are

Write each word once.

he _____   on _____

for _____   are _____

was _____

Scrambled Words

 Unscramble the letters below to make the list words.

1. hyet __ __ __ __

2. sa __ __

3. ta __ __

4. hsi __ __ __

5. iwht __ __ __ __

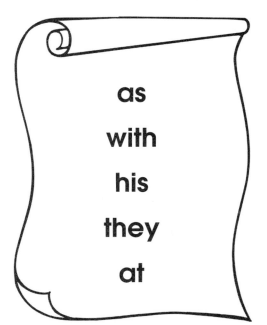

as

with

his

they

at

 Challenge

Use the list words to complete this note.

Hey, Mom!

Dad is _____ Ben. _____ are _____ the store.

I saw Dad take _____ phone _____ he left. Give

him a call.

Me

Name _____

Copy & Circle

Read each word below. Copy it. Then circle the word in the sentence.

| as |
| with |
| his |
| they |
| at |

Read.   Copy.   Circle.

1. as   **1.** _____   **1.** I'll be there as soon as I can.

2. with   **2.** _____   **2.** Come with me to the movie.

3. his   **3.** _____   **3.** Sam took his dog for a walk.

4. they   **4.** _____   **4.** They are best friends.

5. at   **5.** _____   **5.** I left my hat at school.

 Challenge

Circle four of the list words in the story below.

Pie-Eating Contest

Our town had a contest. Who could eat a pie the fastest? The pie eaters sat at a long table. They ate as fast as they could. My dad won! His pie was all gone in 5 minutes!

Hidden Picture

 Color all the shapes that have list words. What picture do you see?

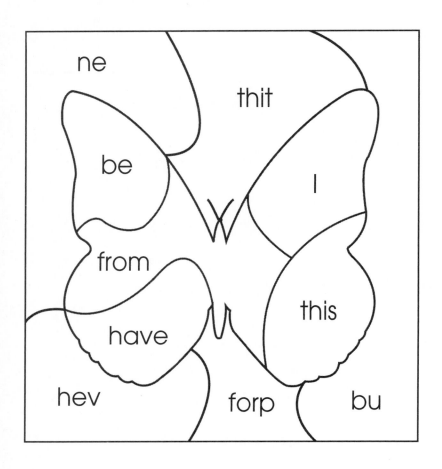

be = yellow

this = orange

from = green

I = pink

have = red

Draw a line to match the list words.

be	have
this	I
from	this
I	be
have	from

Scholastic Success With Sight Words

Name _____

Copy & Circle

 Read each word below. Copy it. Then circle the word in the sentence.

Read.   Copy.   Circle.

1. be   **1.** _____   **1.** Pam will be at the mall.

2. this   **2.** _____   **2.** Is this your house?

3. from   **3.** _____   **3.** He walked home from school.

4. I   **4.** _____   **4.** Matt and I played catch.

5. have   **5.** _____   **5.** How many pets do you have?

 ## Challenge

Circle each of the list words in the note below.

A Note From Nana

To: Nick

From: Nana

I got this from my book store. If you have it, tell me.

It can be returned!

Code Words

 Use this code to write the list words on the lines below.

a ✖   d ★   h ▲   o ●   t ◆
b ♥   e ➤   n ✔   r ■   y ◗

1. ●   ✔   ➤

   ___   ___   ___

2. ♥   ◗

   ___   ___

3. ✔   ●   ◆

   ___   ___   ___

4. ●   ■

   ___   ___

5. ▲   ✖   ★

   ___   ___   ___

or

by

one

had

not

Write each word once.

or   _____   had   _____

by   _____   not   _____

one _____

Word Search

Circle the words from the word list. The words go across and down.

be	from	have	one	this
by	had	not	or	

b k e t h i s g c f

e b x g p r n o i r

f m j a k f o t n o

a e o i r v r b q m

h b h a d l d y u l

m d a k p k f a h d

i n v c g b l j e f

o n e i n s m d z d

p h a c o w b y i n

f c l h t d o l a b

Name _____

What's Missing?

 Fill in the boxes below to make the list words.

1. w h [ ] t

2. b [ ] t

3. [ ] h e n

4. w [ ] r e

5. [ ] l l

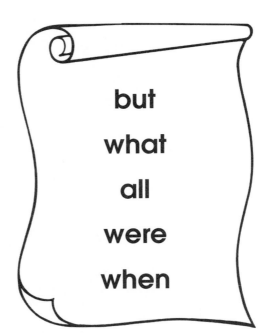

but

what

all

were

when

 Challenge

Fill in the sentences below with list words.

1. She used _____ the eggs.

2. Tell me _____ the party is.

3. I want to go, _____ I am busy.

4. The ducks _____ wet.

5. _____ did you say?

Hidden Picture

 Color all the shapes that have list words.
What picture do you see?

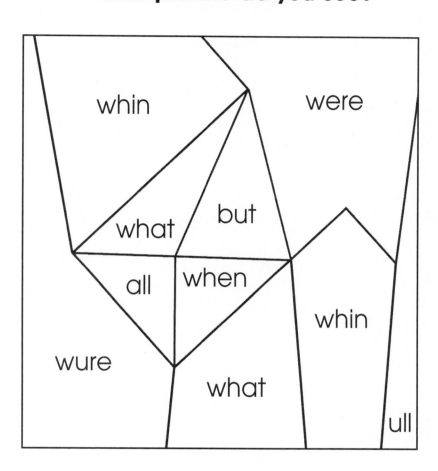

whin

were

what

but

all

when

wure

whin

what

ull

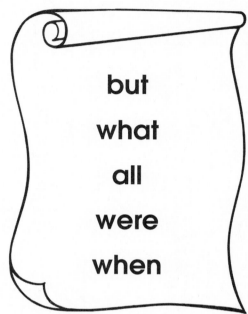

but

what

all

were

when

Write each word once. Circle the words that start with "wh-."

but _____

what _____

all _____

were _____

when _____

Scrambled Words

 Unscramble the letters below to make the list words.

1. anc _ _ _

2. na _ _

3. ereth _ _ _ _ _

4. yuro _ _ _ _

5. ew _ _

we

there

can

an

your

 Challenge

Circle the list words in the ad below.

Garage Sale!

Tons of stuff for sale.

Toys, clothes, books, dishes… even an oven!

We can meet all your needs.

Be there!

Code Words

 Use this code to write the list words on the lines below.

a ✖   e ★   n ▲   r ●   u ◆   y ✚

c ♥   h ➤   o ✔   t ■   w ◗

1. ♥   ✖   ▲

    ___ ___ ___

2. ◗   ★

    ___ ___

3. ✚   ✔   ◆   ●

    ___ ___ ___ ___

4. ✖   ▲

    ___ ___

5. ■   ➤   ★   ●   ★

    ___ ___ ___ ___ ___

we
there
can
an
your

Write each word once.

we _____   an _____

there _____   your _____

can _____

Name _____

Copy & Circle

Read each word below. Copy it. Then circle the word in the sentence.

which
their
said
if
do

Read.   Copy.   Circle.

1. which   **1.** _____   **1.** Which box do you want?

2. their   **2.** _____   **2.** They took their time.

3. said   **3.** _____   **3.** She said she was sorry.

4. if   **4.** _____   **4.** We can stop if you get tired.

5. do   **5.** _____   **5.** What do you want to eat?

Challenge

Circle each of the list words in the note below.

Road Trip

This summer, I took a long car trip with my grandparents. They got two flat tires in one day! Their car was stuck on the road forever, which was not fun. My grandfather said if we do it again, we're taking the train!

Word Search

Circle the words from the word list. The words go across and down.

can	if	their	we	your
do	said	there	which	

e	h	q	k	x	c	s	u	o	b
n	a	y	a	w	h	i	c	h	w
i	d	o	m	g	b	d	a	u	h
r	e	u	v	p	u	o	z	f	l
s	n	r	e	y	c	t	p	r	c
t	l	e	g	s	a	i	d	r	x
h	r	b	v	i	n	t	r	f	a
e	j	i	f	j	a	i	n	c	w
i	g	p	s	h	t	h	e	r	e
r	w	d	o	y	n	z	m	y	t

Word Shapes

 Write words from your word list in the boxes below. The boxes show you the shape of the letters.

1.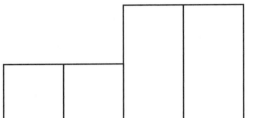

2.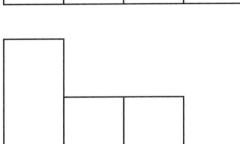

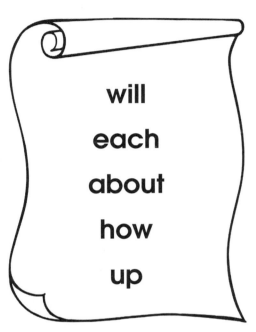

will

each

about

how

up

3.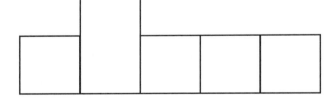

4.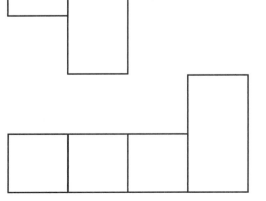

5.

Hidden Picture

 **Color all the shapes that have list words.
What picture do you see?**

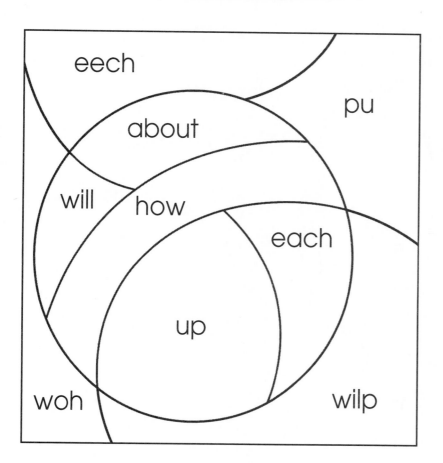

eech

pu

about

will   how

each

up

woh   wilp

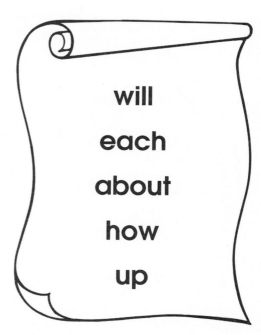

will

each

about

how

up

Draw a line to match the list words.

will	about
each	will
about	how
how	up
up	each

Name _____

What's Missing?

 Complete the sentences by using a letter from the magnifying glass to make a list word.

o   y

e   h

n

out

them

then

she

many

1. Can Henry come _____ut to play?

2. Eat first and the_____ we will go to town.

3. How man_____ pets do you have?

4. Please put th_____m away when you are done.

5. Does s_____e go to camp with you?

Going Places

 Help the bird find its eggs. Connect a path by coloring each nest with a list word.

	many	about	
if	which	then	she
how	up	there	out
if	which	many	an
can	then	will	we
your	them	if	you
each	will	she	(eggs)

Word Shapes

 Write words from your word list in the boxes below.
The boxes show you the shape of the letters.

1.

2.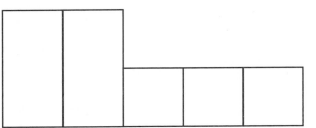

some

so

these

would

other

3.

4.

5.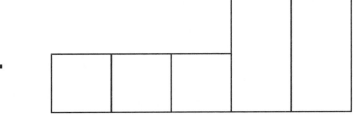

Scrambled Words

 Unscramble the letters below to make the list words.

1. eesht _ _ _ _ _

2. threo _ _ _ _ _

3. os _ _

4. mose _ _ _ _

5. wulod _ _ _ _ _

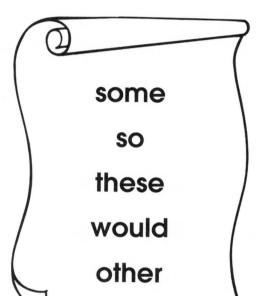

some

so

these

would

other

 Challenge

Use the list words to complete these rhymes.

1. "Put _____ socks on," said his mother.
   "Here is one, and here's the _____."

2. "Spinach, carrots, broccoli, cheese,
   I won't have a bite of _____."

3. "You're _____ silly that you _____
   forget your head, if you could."

Code Words

 Use this code to write the list words on the lines below.

a ✖	h ★	m ▲	o ●	s ◆	w ✚
e ♥	i ➤	n ✔	r ■	t ◗	

1. ➤ ✔ ◗ ●

____ ____ ____ ____

2. ◗ ✚ ●

____ ____ ____

3. ▲ ● ■ ♥

____ ____ ____ ____

4. ★ ♥ ■

____ ____ ____

5. ★ ✖ ◆

____ ____ ____

into

has

more

her

two

Draw a line to match the list words.

into	has
has	more
more	two
her	into
two	her

Name _____

Star Starters

 Begin at the star. Follow the directions. Then write the circled letters on the blanks to spell a list word.

Circle every third letter.

1. ★ g t m u m o d x r v q e

   __ __ __ __

2. ★ b t i m h n e k t s m o

   __ __ __ __

into

has

more

her

two

Circle every fourth letter.

3. ★ m v e h u x s e p a z r

   __ __ __

4. ★ g r c h t y k a q p d s

   __ __ __

5. ★ j w i t o q u w m v y o

   __ __ __

Hidden Picture

 **Color all the shapes that have list words.
What picture do you see?**

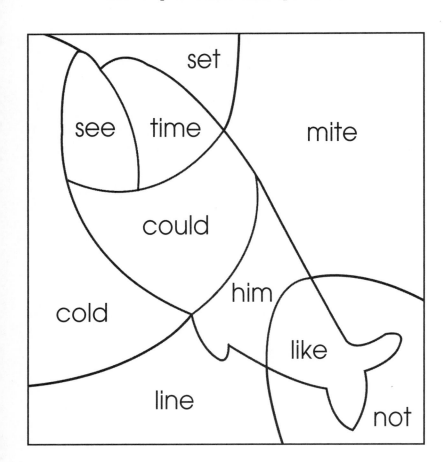

set

see time

mite

could

him

cold

like

line

not

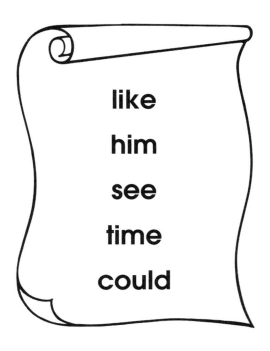

like

him

see

time

could

Write each word once.

like _____

him _____

see _____

time _____

could _____

Word Search

 **Circle the words from the word list.
The words go across and down.**

could	like	see	some	time
him	other	so	these	would

w f b k l o e p s o

o l u n v i l m o r

u s e e t h t o m p

l k r w u l i k e l

d d y b r a m l g q

z o a o t h e r x e

t h e s e h p b l f

y i d k b i f g w e

c m v l o c o u l d

r u e t b a f y t e

What's Missing?

 Complete the sentences by using a letter from the magnifying glass to make a list word.

no

make

than

first

been

1. I am going to ma_____e dinner tonight.

2. She won fi_____st place in the race.

3. There are n_____ clouds in the sky.

4. Have you ever b_____en to the park?

5. I'd rather eat an apple th_____n a banana.

Name _____

Copy & Circle

Read each word below. Copy it. Then circle the word in the sentence.

no
make
than
first
been

Read.   Copy.   Circle.

1. no

1. _____

1. There are no bugs at the lake.

2. make

2. _____

2. Birds make nests in that tree.

3. than

3. _____

3. She'd rather play than work.

4. first

4. _____

4. She ran to first base.

5. been

5. _____

5. How have you been?

 Challenge

Circle each of the list words in the to-do list below.

My To-Do List!

1. First, make my bed (and Ben has to make his own).
2. Clean playroom (even though it's Ben's mess more than mine!).
3. Put away clothes that have been folded (by Ben!).
4. Be sure there are no weeds in garden. (Ben's job is to weed).

Star Starters

 Begin at the star. Follow the directions. Then write the circled letters on the blanks to spell a list word.

Circle every other letter.

1. i p u e t o r p m l w e

__ __ __ __ __ __

Circle every fourth letter.

2. b v a m p o g y k

__ __ __

its

who

now

people

my

Circle every third letter.

3. l z w y s h x m o k c

__ __ __

4. p w i a j t i c s

__ __ __

5. m d n r e o s y w

__ __ __

Scrambled Words

 Unscramble the letters below to make the list words.

1. sti __ __ __

2. onw __ __ __

3. ym __ __

4. woh __ __ __

5. eelopp __ __ __ __ __ __

its

who

now

people

my

 Challenge

Use four of the list words to complete this email.

To: lizb@email.com
From: me
Subject: B'day Party

I can't wait for _____ birthday party. I still don't know _____ is coming. There might be 22 _____! As of _____, there will be 17 guests.

See you soon!
Me

Hidden Picture

 Color all the shapes that have list words. What picture do you see?

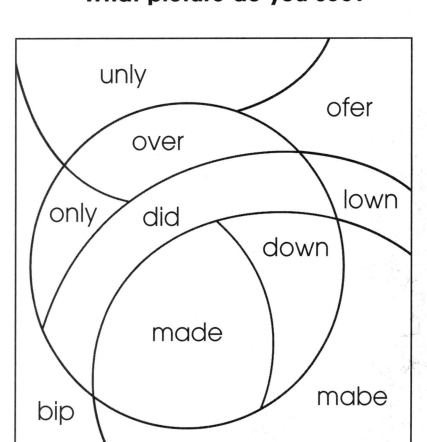

unly

ofer

over

only   did

lown

down

made

bip

mabe

made

over

did

down

only

Extra!

Draw a picture to show the list word *down*.

Name _____

Going Places

 Help the boy reach the basket. Connect a path by coloring each ball with a list word.

made
over
did
down
only

can

over

made

only

he

did

down

did

over

made

over

then

only

how

START

Word Shapes

 Write words from your word list in the boxes below. The boxes show you the shape of the letters.

1.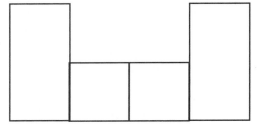

2.

3.

4.

5.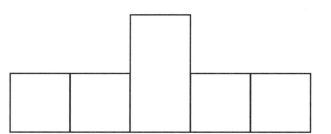

way

find

use

may

water

Code Words

 Use this code to write the list words on the lines below.

a ✖   e ★   i ▲   n ●   s ◆   u ✚   y ✳

d ♥   f ➤   m ✔   r ■   t ◗   w ✿

1. ✿   ✖   ✳

___ ___ ___

2. ✚   ◆   ★

___ ___ ___

3. ✔   ✖   ✳

___ ___ ___

4. ✿   ✖   ◗   ★   ■

___ ___ ___ ___ ___

5. ➤   ▲   ●   ♥

___ ___ ___ ___

> way
> find
> use
> may
> water

Draw a line to match the list words.

way   find

find   use

use   may

may   water

water   way

Name _____

Connect It!

 Connect the letters in the first column with letters in the second to make list words. Then write the word next to the numbers below.

1. lo   ter

2. wo   tle

3. lit   ng

4. af   ry

5. ve   rds

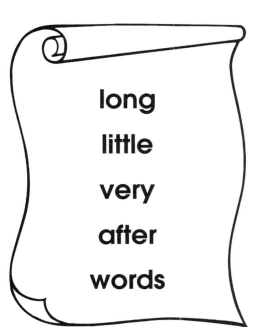

long

little

very

after

words

1. _____

2. _____

3. _____

4. _____

5. _____

Name _____

Scrambled Words

 Unscramble the letters below to make the list words.

1. lttile _ _ _ _ _ _

2. wrdos _ _ _ _ _

3. ratef _ _ _ _ _

4. evyr _ _ _ _

5. lgon _ _ _ _

long

little

very

after

words

 Challenge

Use four of the list words to complete this email.

Dear Maria,

This is just a _____ note to thank you for helping at

the bake sale. You were there for a _____ _____

time! _____ the sale, we had enough money for our

class trip. There are no _____ to thank you enough!

Name _____

Star Starters

 Begin at the star. Follow the directions. Then write the circled letters on the blanks to spell a list word.

Circle every other letter.

1. b c p a m l f l x e w d

___ ___ ___ ___ ___ ___

2. g w l h o e a r t e

___ ___ ___ ___ ___

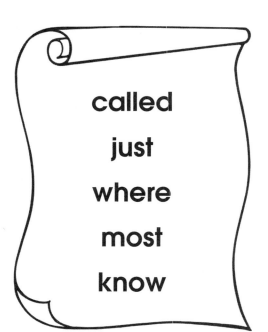
called

just

where

most

know

Circle every third letter.

3. m h k f z n p y o e s w

___ ___ ___ ___

4. v c m c z o l t s j i t

___ ___ ___ ___

★
5. l c j r w u x m s p o t

___ ___ ___ ___

Name _____

Hidden Picture

 Color all the shapes that have list words.
What picture do you see?

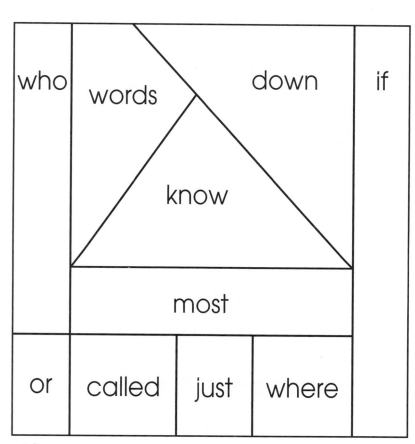

called
just
where
most
know

 Challenge

Find four list words in the note below.

Mom,

Dad just called to ask where his shoes are. Do you know?

Me

Inside box words: who, words, down, if, know, most, or, called, just, where

Word Search

 Circle the words from the word list. The words go across and down.

about	from	one	there	which
and	have	that	was	with
are	his	the	were	you
each	not	their	what	your

```
r  s  t  m  v  o  e  l  y  w  a  s  w
h  a  r  e  i  t  h  l  b  e  p  r  h
o  t  s  a  z  p  f  w  n  r  u  c  g
h  j  d  c  s  r  r  a  k  e  n  l  s
w  v  b  h  a  b  o  u  t  k  t  h  t
h  e  r  e  n  c  m  c  g  h  o  b  h
a  a  l  n  d  n  t  e  y  o  u  r  a
t  g  p  m  n  e  h  a  o  t  h  t  t
h  c  t  h  e  r  e  l  u  b  d  h  t
m  i  u  g  d  k  i  s  v  x  q  e  w
o  n  e  o  n  t  r  u  h  a  v  e  i
y  o  o  r  e  f  m  t  i  e  j  e  t
a  t  w  h  i  c  h  h  s  t  r  v  h
```

Name _____

Word Search

 Circle the words from the word list. The words go across and down.

been	into	make	out	time
called	know	more	over	water
down	like	now	people	words
find	little	other	them	would

```
a  c  l  f  i  n  d  q  h  p  r  w
j  t  i  m  e  l  d  u  s  t  w  o
n  h  n  k  a  o  c  h  m  i  o  u
c  e  t  h  c  f  a  e  a  b  r  l
e  m  o  r  e  m  l  i  k  e  d  d
l  i  d  b  a  h  l  o  e  u  s  e
i  p  e  o  p  l  e  j  s  g  y  k
t  g  t  v  x  l  d  q  u  n  a  n
t  b  e  e  n  k  n  o  w  o  u  t
l  n  r  r  p  d  e  z  c  w  r  v
e  i  l  s  w  a  t  e  r  o  i  f
o  t  h  e  r  m  s  n  d  o  w  n
```

100 Words List

a	find	know	out	two
about	first	like	over	up
after	for	little	people	use
all	from	long	said	very
an	had	made	see	was
and	has	make	she	water
are	have	many	so	way
as	he	may	some	we
at	her	more	than	were
be	him	most	that	what
been	his	my	the	when
but	how	no	their	where
by	I	not	them	which
called	if	now	then	who
can	in	of	there	will
could	into	on	these	with
did	is	one	they	words
do	it	only	this	would
down	its	or	time	you
each	just	other	to	your

Answer Key

PAGE 4
1. to 2. of 3. and 4. a 5. the

Challenge
1. of 2. a 3. and 4. the

PAGE 6
you, is, that, it, in

Challenge
Thank <u>you</u> for the hat. <u>It is</u> just what I wanted. I hope <u>that</u> I will see you in the summer.

PAGE 7
Did <u>you</u> know <u>that</u> some turtles can live a very long time? One turtle <u>in</u> South America <u>is</u> over 240 years old. <u>It is</u> a very old turtle.

PAGE 8
1. was 2. for 3. are 4. he 5. on

Challenge
1. was 2. are 3. for 4. on 5. he

PAGE 9
1. for 2. on 3. was 4. he 5. are

PAGE 10
1. they 2. as 3. at 4. his 5. with

Challenge
Hey, Mom! Dad is <u>with</u> Ben. <u>They</u> are <u>at</u> the store. I saw Dad took <u>his</u> phone <u>as</u> he left. Give him a call. Me

PAGE 11
Our town had a contest. Who could eat a pie the fastest? The pie eaters sat <u>at</u> a long table with lots of pies. They ate <u>as</u> fast <u>as</u> <u>they</u> could. My dad won! <u>His</u> pie was all gone in 5 minutes!

PAGE 13

Challenge
To: Nick <u>From</u>: Nana
<u>I</u> got <u>this</u> <u>from</u> my book store. If you <u>have</u> it, tell me. It can <u>be</u> returned!

PAGE 14
1. one 2. by 3. not 4. or 5. had

PAGE 15

PAGE 16
1. what 2. but 3. when 4. were 5. all

Challenge
1. all 2. when 3. but 4. were 5. what

PAGE 18
1. can 2. an 3. there 4. your 5. we

Challenge
Tons of stuff for sale. Toys, clothes, books, dishes… even <u>an</u> oven! <u>We</u> <u>can</u> meet all <u>your</u> needs. Be <u>there</u>!

PAGE 19
1. can 2. we 3. your 4. an 5. there

PAGE 20

Challenge
This summer, I took a long car trip with my grandparents. They got two flat tires in one day! <u>Their</u> car was stuck on the road forever, <u>which</u> was not fun. My grandfather <u>said</u> <u>if</u> we <u>do</u> it again, we're taking the train!

PAGE 21

Answer Key

PAGE 22
1. will 2. how 3. about 4. up 5. each

PAGE 24
1. out 2. then 3. many 4. them 5. she

PAGE 26
1. so 2. these 3. some 4. other 5. would

PAGE 27
1. these 2. other 3. so 4. some 5. would

Challenge
1. some, other 2. these 3. so, would

PAGE 28
1. into 2. two 3. more 4. her 5. has

PAGE 29
1. more 2. into 3. her 4. has 5. two

PAGE 31

```
w  f  b  k  l  o  e  p  s  o
o  l  u  n  v  i  l  m  o  r
u  s  e  e  t  h  t  o  m  p
l  k  r  w  u  l  i  k  e  l
d  d  y  b  r  a  m  l  g  q
   z  o  a  o  t  h  e  r  x  e
   t  h  e  s  e  h  p  b  l  f
y  i  d  k  b  i  f  g  w  e
c  m  v  l  o  c  o  u  l  d
r  u  e  t  b  a  f  y  t  e
```

PAGE 32
1. make 2. first 3. no 4. been 5. than

PAGE 33

Challenge
1. first, make, make 2. than 3. been 4. no

PAGE 34
1. people 2. my 3. who 4. its 5. now

PAGE 35
1. its 2. now 3. my 4. who 5. people

Challenge
I can't wait for <u>my</u> birthday party. I still don't know <u>who</u> is coming. There might be 22 <u>people</u>! As of <u>now</u>, there will be 17 guests.

PAGE 38
1. find 2. way 3. use 4. may 5. water
Note: <u>way</u> and <u>may</u> are transposable.

PAGE 39
1. way 2. use 3. may 4. water 5. find

PAGE 40
1. long 2. words 3. little 4. after 5. very

PAGE 41
1. little 2. words 3. after 4. very 5. long

Challenge
This is just a <u>little</u> note to thank you for helping at the bake sale. You were there for a <u>very long</u> time! <u>After</u> the sale, we had enough money for our class trip. There are no <u>words</u> to thank you enough!

PAGE 42
1. called 2. where 3. know 4. most 5. just

PAGE 43

Challenge
Dad <u>just called</u> to ask <u>where</u> his shoes are. Do you <u>know</u>?

PAGE 44

```
r  s  t  m  v  o  e  l  y  w  a  s  w
h  a  r  e  i  t  h  l  b  e  p  r  h
o  t  s  a  z  p  f  w  n  r  u  c  g
h  j  d  c  s  r  r  a  k  e  n  l  s
w  v  b  h  a  b  o  u  t  k  t  h  t
h  e  r  e  n  c  m  c  g  h  o  b  h
a  a  l  n  d  n  t  e  y  o  u  r  a
t  g  p  m  n  e  h  a  o  t  h  t  t
h  c  t  h  e  r  e  l  u  b  d  h  t
m  i  u  g  d  k  i  s  v  x  q  e  w
o  n  e  o  n  t  r  u  h  a  v  e  i
y  o  o  r  e  f  m  t  i  e  j  e  t
a  t  w  h  i  c  h  h  s  t  r  v  h
```

PAGE 45

```
a  c  l  f  i  n  d  q  h  p  r  w
j  t  i  m  e  l  d  u  s  t  w  o
n  h  n  k  a  o  c  h  m  i  o  u
c  e  t  h  c  f  a  e  a  b  r  l
e  m  o  r  e  m  l  i  k  e  d  d
l  i  d  b  a  h  l  o  e  u  s  e
i  p  e  o  p  l  e  j  s  g  y  k
t  g  t  v  x  l  d  q  u  n  a  n
t  b  e  e  n  k  n  o  w  o  u  t
l  n  r  r  p  d  e  z  c  w  r  v
e  i  l  s  w  a  t  e  r  o  i  f
o  t  h  e  r  m  s  n  d  o  w  n
```